First World War
and Army of Occupation
War Diary
France, Belgium and Germany

25 DIVISION
75 Infantry Brigade
Gloucestershire Regiment
1/5th Battalion (Territorial)
1 September 1918 - 28 February 1919

WO95/2251/1

Published by

The Naval & Military Press Ltd

Unit 10 Ridgewood Industrial Park,

Uckfield, East Sussex,

TN22 5QE England

Tel: +44 (0) 1825 749494

www.naval-military-press.com

www.nmarchive.com

This diary has been reprinted in facsimile from the original. Any imperfections are inevitably reproduced and the quality may fall short of modern type and cartographic standards.

© Crown Copyright
Images reproduced by permission of The National Archives, London, England, 2015.

Contents

Document type	Place/Title	Date From	Date To
Heading	WO95/2251-1		
Heading	25th Division 75th Infy Bde 1-5th Bn Gloster Regt Sep 1918-Feb 1919		
Miscellaneous	75th Inf Bde	26/11/1918	26/11/1918
War Diary	Club Camp	01/09/1918	02/09/1918
War Diary	In Support	03/09/1918	06/09/1918
War Diary	In The Line	07/09/1918	11/09/1918
War Diary	Granezza	12/09/1918	12/09/1918
War Diary	Centrale	13/09/1918	14/09/1918
War Diary	En Route	15/09/1918	17/09/1918
War Diary	Domvast	18/09/1918	27/09/1918
War Diary	Warloy	28/09/1918	29/09/1918
War Diary	Montauban	30/09/1918	30/09/1918
War Diary		01/09/1918	21/09/1918
Heading	1/5th Battn. Gloucestershire Regt. War Diary Volume XLIII		
War Diary	Montauban	01/10/1918	01/10/1918
War Diary	Leuze Wood	02/10/1918	02/10/1918
War Diary	Nurlu	03/10/1918	03/10/1918
War Diary	S Emilie	04/10/1918	04/10/1918
War Diary	Quennemont	05/10/1918	06/10/1918
War Diary	In The Line	07/10/1918	11/10/1918
War Diary	Honnechy	12/10/1918	12/10/1918
War Diary	Serain	13/10/1918	18/10/1918
War Diary	In The Line	19/10/1918	24/10/1918
War Diary	Pommereuil	25/10/1918	30/10/1918
War Diary	Malgarni	31/10/1918	31/10/1918
Heading	1/5th Battn Gloucestershire Regt War Diary Vol. XLIV		
War Diary	In The Line Malgarni	01/11/1918	04/11/1918
War Diary	In The Line	04/11/1918	08/11/1918
War Diary	Preux Au Bois	09/11/1918	13/11/1918
War Diary	Le Cateau	14/11/1918	27/11/1918
War Diary	Carnieres	29/11/1918	30/11/1918
War Diary	War Diary For Month Of December 1918 Vol. 42		
War Diary	Carnieres	01/12/1918	16/12/1918
War Diary	Cambrai	17/12/1918	31/12/1918
Miscellaneous	Honours And Awards	27/12/1918	27/12/1918
Heading	1/5th Bn Gloucestershire Regiment War Diary For Month Of January 1919 Vol. 43		
War Diary	Cambrai	01/01/1919	31/01/1919
Heading	1/5th Battn. Gloucestershire Regt. War Diary Volume XLVIII		
War Diary	Cambrai	01/02/1919	28/02/1919

WO 95/2251/1

25TH DIVISION
75TH INFY BDE

1-5TH BN GLOSTER REGT
SEP 1918 - FEB 1919

(FROM 48 DIV. 145 BRIGADE
ITALY)

and same Div France from
1915 DEC MAR – 1917 OCT

75th Inf. Bde

Herewith copy of WAR DIARY for
month of September 1918 as requested.

Lieut Colonel
Cmd'g 1/5 Bn Gloucestershire
Reg't

GR53
26-11-18

Sep '18
/
Feb '19

Army Form C. 2118.

Copy 15/75 Sept 1918 Vol 43

WAR DIARY
or
INTELLIGENCE SUMMARY.
(Erase heading not required.)

42 O Sheet

Place	Date	Hour	Summary of Events and Information	Remarks and references to Appendices
CLUB CAMP	1-9-18		Divine Service 8.30am - 11.0am. Church Parade for remainder ex Camp at 11.30	
	2-9-18		Inspection of Camp by C.O. Lewis Gun Competition afternoon & evening won by B Coy. Divine occasional meet. The Battn relieved 1/7 Worcesters in Left Support Right Sub. Disposition Right to Left A B C D Coys. The Battn returned Rainbow by order of Bde.	
IN SUPPORT	3-9-18		Divine Work on Coy areas. D Coy building huts.	
	4-9-18		Divine Work on Coy areas & training under O.C. Coys. D Coy building huts.	
	5-9-18		Divine Training under OC Coys. D Coy building huts. Whilst in Support there was very little shelling except on night of 5/6th when a few shells fell around Bn HQ & in B Coy Area.	
	6-9-18		Divine The Battn relieved the 1/4th Oxford Bucks in the line opposite Ave. Dispositions A Coy Right Outpost Line of Resistance. D Coy Left " " " " B Coy Support in Major Fassa Switch. C Coy Reserve. 1 Platoon fraquet line by day. " " " " " night. 2nd Lt H.G. Powell and 1 Platton proceeded on patrol to S. Ave which was found to be occupied. The patrol harrassed the enemy with LG at intervals till 2.0 am	

WAR DIARY
or
INTELLIGENCE SUMMARY

Army Form C. 2118.

Place	Date	Hour	Summary of Events and Information	Remarks and references to Appendices
In the Line	7-9-18		June. Trench routine work by Coys on their areas. 2nd Lt C F HUSSEY + 1 Platoon started at 1 am patrolled to S AVE. The patrol, after a short preliminary bombardment on Ronces by Artillery, occupied houses, remaining there until 2.30 am. The enemy moved off and did not return.	
	8-9-18		June. Trench routine. Patrols Lt P A MORFEY and 1 Platoon. The patrol proceeded towards S AVE at 8.40 pm. The enemy was found to be holding S AVE. On advancing the patrol was engaged by enemy at the same time our artillery opened fire on S AVE as per arrangement. N.S. known 1 L.G. artillery ceased the patrol advanced and occupied houses until 10.30 pm. The shower remained there until 5.0 am. Nothing further was heard of the enemy.	
	9-9-18		June. Trench routine. The 2nd Durhams and 1/5th Warwicks raided the enemy lines at 11.30 pm + 1/4 Oxfords at 4.0 pm. The Oxfords captured 37 prisoners + 2 MG's. During the raid the Padre Rev C A Clark. MC was badly burned by falling rock outside the Dressing Station.	
	10-9-18		June. Wet night. Trench routine. Patrols cancelled at last moment 11.30 pm. Orders received that the Battn was to be relieved that it would proceed to FRANCE to form 2nd Div.	
	11-9-18		Misty morning June. The Battn proceeded to GRANEZZA by 3.30 pm.	
GRANEZZA	12-9-18		June. The Battn proceeded down the mountains to CENTRALE near THIENE. The Battn the relief being complete.	

Army Form C. 2118.

WAR DIARY
or
INTELLIGENCE SUMMARY.
(Erase heading not required.)

Place	Date	Hour	Summary of Events and Information	Remarks and references to Appendices
GRANEZZA	12-9-18		arrived here by 1.30pm. 25th Divisional Camp.	
			Composition of 25th Div.	
			1/5TH GLOUCESTER ⎫	
			1/8 " WORCESTER ⎬ drawn 48th Div to form 75th Bde.	
			1/8 " WARWICKS ⎭	
			9th DEVONS ⎫	
			20 " MANCHESTERS ⎬ drawn 7th Div to form 7th Bde	
			21st " ⎭	
			11th SHERWOODS ⎫	
			9th YORKS ⎬ drawn 23rd Div to form 7th Bde.	
			13th DURHAM L.I. ⎭	
CENTRALE	13-9-18		Bn. Preparations for entraining.	
	14-9-18		Bn. The Battn. entrained at THIENE. 1st train at 3.30am 2nd 6.40am.	
EN ROUTE	15-9-18		Bn. Crossed FRENCH FRONTIER at MODANE at the morning of the 15th R. Detrained at St RIQUIER	
	16 to 17-9-18		(N. ABBEVILLE) by 10am morning of 17th R. The Battn. marched 4½ miles into billets at DOMVAST_	
			in billets by 1.30 pm. Billets Barns + outhouses roomy.	
DOMVAST	18-9-18		Bn. Route march of 8 miles in morning through CRECY WOOD.	
			Lewis Gunners, Scouts, Stretcher Bearers Special instruction during afternoon.	
DOMVAST	19-9-18		Bn. Drill Demonstration to Officers + NCOs. Companies cleaning + fitting equipment	

Army Form C. 2118.

WAR DIARY
or
INTELLIGENCE SUMMARY.
(Erase heading not required.)

Instructions regarding War Diaries and Intelligence Summaries are contained in F. S. Regs., Part II. and the Staff Manual respectively. Title pages will be prepared in manuscript.

Place	Date	Hour	Summary of Events and Information	Remarks and references to Appendices
DOMVAST	20-9-18		The Divisional Band Officer lectured Companies on Gas XI the morning & Officers in the Afternoon. Special instruction to Lewis Gunners, Scouts & Stretcher Bearers for 1 hour in afternoon.	
	21-9-18		Inve 9-10.15 am Platoon Coy Drill, 10.15-12.30 Coys under Coy Commanders. Specialists under S.O. 9-12.30 am Specialist classes as above. Church Inspection by G.O.C. Bde in morning. Battalion Mass followed by a March Past. The G.O.C. commented on the following:- 1. The very good turn out. 2. Great steadiness on parade. 3. Cleanliness of mens equipment. 4. Good condition of transport. Specialist classes as above.	
	22-9-18		Inve. C of E Church Parade 11.15am. Scabies inspection by M.O. during morning.	
	23-9-18		Inve. A Coy Lewis Gun Range. Remainder on individual training. 9-12.30am B C & D Coys Coy Drill & Platoon Attack. The Div General visited training area. Specialist classes as above. Steel helmet covers abolished.	
DOMVAST	24-9-18		Showery. A & D Coys 9-11.15am Coy Drill & attack formation 11.30-12.30 P.C. classes individual training.	

WAR DIARY
or
INTELLIGENCE SUMMARY.
(Erase heading not required.)

Army Form C. 2118.

Place	Date	Hour	Summary of Events and Information	Remarks and references to Appendices
			B Coy Lewis Gun Range 7am - 1pm.	
			C " " " " from 1pm.	
			Specialist classes as above. The Battn was made up to strength establishment of Lewis Guns ie 36 - 8 per Coy + 8 Battn HQ.	
DOMVAST	25-9-18		Coys A B + D Coy passed through Gas Chamber. Training Close order drill + attack formation.	
			Specialist classes as above. 1st Line Transport proceeded to WARLOY near ALBERT by road — 3 days march.	
	26-9-18		Coys A B Coy Lewis Gun Range. 8th Reserve Coy at disposal of O.C. Coys.	
	27-9-18		Coys The Battn marched to ST RIQUIER entraining at 3.30pm for ALBERT detraining at midnight. The Battn marched 6 miles to WARLOY arriving in billets at 2.30am. The billets were good barns slightly damaged by shell fire	
WARLOY	28-9-18		Reserve Coy at disposal of O.C. Coys.	
	29-9-18		Coys. The Battn embussed at 12 noon for MONTAUBAN arriving in camp 2.30pm. Camp manager 16 bivouac huts and dugouts. Heavy wet night.	
MONTAUBAN	30-9-18		Normal Company training + reorganisation of platoons. Owing to shortage of men the Battn reverted to three platoons per Company — the HQs of the 14th Platoon per Coy to be drawn from	

WAR DIARY
or
INTELLIGENCE SUMMARY.
(Erase heading not required.)

Army Form C. 2118.

Summary of Events and Information

...in the event of operations to form a nucleus on the arrival of a large draft.

During the past month there was very little sickness. Reinforcements complained during hike.

WEEKLY STATES.

WEEK ENDING	TOTAL RATIONED	ANIMALS	VEHICLES 2 WHEELED	4 WHEELED
7/9/18	578	75	4	13
14/9/18	627	55	4	14
21/9/18	623	55	4	14
28/9/18	609	55	4	14

CASUALTIES.
9/9/18 — 1 OR Wounded in action
" — 1 OR " (at duty)
12/9/18 — Rev C.A.Clark, MC Wounded in action (at duty)

HOSPITAL

ADMITTED
36 OR during month

DISCHARGED
8 OR during month

COURSES.

6/9/18	2 OR to H.R.Div Signal School (at Conrae)	8/9/18 — 1 OR rejoined from I.H.Q Sounds Course
7/9/18	2 OR rejoined from I.H.R.Div School Staff	" — 1 OR " Signal School
9/9/18	1 OR " G.H.Q General Course	" — 1 OR " Corps Lewis Guns Course
	1 OR " "	" — 1 OR " Stokes Mortar "
	1 OR " Corps Lewis	17/9/18 — 8 OR " G.H.Q Signal Course
	1 OR " G.H.Q Gas	" — 2 OR " H.S Div "

Army Form C. 2118.

WAR DIARY
or
INTELLIGENCE SUMMARY.
(Erase heading not required.)

Place	Date	Hour	Summary of Events and Information	Remarks and references to Appendices
			MOVES of OFFICERS.	
	1/9/18		Capt A.T. MITCHESON Taken on strength of category "B" Officers struck of strength of Bath.	
			Lieut J.A. CARROL Granted 14 days leave to ENGLAND.	
			Capt C.O.H. SEWELL To 48th Divl HQ from 145 Bde HQ	
	4/9/18		P.C. HILL Granted 7 days leave to LAKE GARDA.	
	7/9/18		2/Lieut J.E. ROBERTS To ENGLAND for transfer to R.A.F.	
	11/9/18		Capt V.B. BRISHAM-HALL Granted extension of leave till 16.9.18 on medical grounds.	
	13/9/18		P.C. HILL Rejoined from 7 days leave at LAKE GARDA	
			F.E. FRANCILLON Both from 145 Bde HQ	
			Lieut W. WALKER Transferred to 11th Bucks Bn struck off strength of 1/5 Bn Glos Regt.	
	15/9/18		Capt C.O.H. SEWELL Struck off strgth of 1/5th Bn Glos Regt.	
	16/9/18		2/Lieut H.R.H. MORRIS Granted extension of leave to 18/9/18 on medical grounds.	
	2/9/18		Lieut & QM T. DENNIS Joined Bn on return from duty.	
			2/Lt (a/Capt) G.E. RATCLIFFE M.C. " " "	
			2/Lieut A.J. COX " " "	
			A.H. FEARMAN " " "	
			H.C. LODGE " " "	
	21/9/18		Lieut J.A. CARROLL Granted extension of leave to 8 days (awaiting M.O. A.G.H.Q 27/9/18).	

Signed

Lieut Colonel.
Comdg 1/5 Bn Gloucestershire Regt.

1/5th BATTN: GLOUCESTERSHIRE REGT:

War Diary

VOLUME XLIII

OCTOBER 1918

Army Form C. 2118.

WAR DIARY
or
INTELLIGENCE SUMMARY.
(Erase heading not required.)

Instructions regarding War Diaries and Intelligence Summaries are contained in F.S. Regs., Part II and the Staff Manual respectively. Title pages will be prepared in manuscript.

Place	Date	Hour	Summary of Events and Information	Remarks and references to Appendices
MONTAUBAN	1-10-18		Fine. The Bde. in the morning marched 4 miles to LEUZE WOOD - w/o casualties. The Bn. was accommodated in dugouts & shelters. After tea the Bn. carried out a tactical exercise - Bn. advancing to the attack.	
LEUZE WOOD	2-10-18		Fine. 17.30 hrs. the Bde. marched to NURLU (9 miles) arriving at 17.30 hrs. into billets - [par?] tially damaged houses huts & dug outs. Blankets & surplus stuff was dumped here.	
NURLU	3-10-18		Fine. The Bde. stood by during the morning & moved at 16.45 hrs. to S. EMILIE (5 miles) arriving after dusk at 20.00 hrs. There was no accommodation for the Bde. so it encamped in a field under groundsheets. The night was dry but cold - the men having no blankets.	
S. EMILIE	4-10-18		Fine - fresh. The Bde. stood by with horses in chafflo pile. domn. from 07.00 hrs. till 00 hrs. 11.20 hrs. the Bde. marched to 4 hillsided in the support system of the Hindenburg Line at QUENNEMONT Farm - 1 mile W. of BONY. This system was greatly damaged & contained but few dugouts	
MONT QUENNET	5-10-18		Fine. All great coats haversacks dumped B.Echelon moved back to HARGICOURT. The Bn. marched in fighting order to LORMISSET (4 miles) arriving under occasional shells fire. g.s. whilst passing GRANDCOURT suffering different 5 casualties.	
		15.20	The Bn. took up its position in sunkenroads in support to f/o warriors. who had just	

WAR DIARY
or
INTELLIGENCE SUMMARY.
(Erase heading not required.)

Army Form C. 2118.

Place	Date	Hour	Summary of Events and Information	Remarks and references to Appendices
			Captured BELLEVUE FARM – over looking BEAUREVOIR.	
		16.20	The Batt. recd orders to attack & take BEAUREVOIR which 2 Brigades had failed to take.	
			1/6 WORCESTERS to take N. half & the 1/Glos. to take S. half of the village.	
			Dispositions. A. Coy. Left front) on a front of 200" each.	
			B. " Right ")	
			C. " Support up	
			D. " Reserve	
		16.15	Under cover of a heavy artillery barrage & M.G. fire the Batt. moved into its assemble position.	
		16.40	Under a creeping barrage of 100" per 6' the Batt. advanced towards BEAUREVOIR in Artillery formation. When nearing the Railway Embankment which skirts the WEST of the town A. Coy. from over keen men advanced into our barrage followed by B. Coy. on the left – A Coy suffering several casualties the Coys. were thus able to surprise a M.G. nest holding the embankment, which did its taking several from our barrage (11 M.G.s were afterwards found along this embankment). The Batt. then pushed forward into & thro' the village meeting with very little	

WAR DIARY
or
INTELLIGENCE SUMMARY.
(Erase heading not required.)

Army Form C. 2118.

Place	Date	Hour	Summary of Events and Information	Remarks and references to Appendices
		19.15	Airplane over flew from isolated M.G. Snipers which were quickly mopped up by C. Coy. A line was established 200' East of the town in conjunction with the 1/5 WORCESTERS.	
			Lt. & SEARS seriously wounded by a sniper in the village. 2/Lt. HUSSEY killed by our barrage on the Railway Embankment.	
			Casualties — Killed Wounded 9 OR Killed, 42 " wounded 1 missing	
		4.00 to 6-10-16 01.00	No enemy shells + M.G. fire was heard between these hours — then going the Bath Rifles but from 01.00 the enemy started to shell us & the village with H.E & C.9 shells, eventually bringing aromatic fire upon the whole village & western approaches during the remainder of the day.	
			After dark, Platoon of the 1/5 WORCESTERS Cox with 1 Platoon of C. Coy. under Lt. a further trial on advanced enemy position, but on meeting stubborn resistance from M.G. snipers received casualties the raiders were compelled to withdraw.	
			Casualties — 2 killed, 2 wounded.	

WAR DIARY
or
INTELLIGENCE SUMMARY.
(Erase heading not required.)

Army Form C. 2118.

Place	Date	Hour	Summary of Events and Information	Remarks and references to Appendices
IN THE LINE	7-10-18		Fine. Buzzle in the evening. Heavy shelling on our position & village during morning & evening. The Batt. was relieved by the S. AFRICAN Brigade of the 4th Divsn. at	
"	8-10-18	01-30 hrs.	The Batt. moved to Reinforced N.J. ESTREET arriving at 04-30 hrs with no further casualties.	
			On plan the 3rd Try Armies commenced an attack along the whole front advancing about 5 miles. The 75th Bde. followed up at 04-30 hrs. to PONCHAUX later to SONIA WOOD where it bivouacked the night in the dry bed of the TORRENS CANAL. The Batt. recd orders to attack at 05-20 hrs the following morning. The Batt. on a two fronts with 74th Bde on Right & 24th Divsn on Left in Sqr. to attack under a creeping barrage of 100' for 3 minutes to take up a positn. N.E.J. from the if WORCHETERS. Was then to pass thro' & carry on the attack without a barrage.	
			Disposition D Coy Right front } each on 200 front	
			C " Left " }	
			B " Support }	
			A " Reserve	

WAR DIARY
or
INTELLIGENCE SUMMARY.
(Erase heading not required.)

Army Form C. 2118.

Place	Date	Hour	Summary of Events and Information	Remarks and references to Appendices
IN THE LINE	9-10-18		Fine - mist took an hour or so about 07.30 h.	
		03.20	The Batt. moved into assembly posit. South of SERAIN FARM.	
		05.20	The Barrage opened & at 05.25 "A" Co. & "B" Co. & "C" coy of "D" Co. advanced to take MORETZ. Barrage to be closely supported by the 1/F WORCESTER. The Batt advanced to take MORETZ. to the left the 66. Division had not arrived, neither had 05.45 there a barrage until 05.45 which overlapped onto our sector caused several casualties among the WORCESTER from Suffolk Avenue Coy.	
		06.10	The Barrage of peaceful the town MARETZ having lifted CO by. pushed forward to occupied the W. outskirts of the town. Here the Barrage of the 1/5 Dev. shel 1/5 7 Sh. later shot over the corner & after causing many casualties in C Coy. compelled the forward Coys. to withdraw. After it had lifted the Batt. again pushed forward meeting very little resistance until it reached the E. outskirts of the village where it met with stubborn resistance from M.G. & trifle after some heavy fighting. the Batt acquired the town consolidated under heavy fire 200 - 205° E. of Far. Here the 1/5 WORCESTER passed thro' & eventually the cavalry	

WAR DIARY
or
INTELLIGENCE SUMMARY.
(Erase heading not required.)

Army Form C. 2118.

Place	Date	Hour	Summary of Events and Information	Remarks and references to Appendices
IN THE LINE	10-10-18		Fine. 05:20 the Batt. advanced astride LE CATEAU in artillery formation — to DAWNA, 1st Coys. K. WORCESTER then onto E. of HENNECOURT rendezvous. We met with what gradually stiffened as the WARWICKS advanced — on the WARWICKS Rallying B. hy. was gallantly led forward the 15th War orient by Capt. R de W ROGER but being heavily enfiladed by M. G. fire & having lost all its officers & most many of its N.C.O.'s lay & was forced to fall back upon the WARWICKS when they too gave in. the Batt. having had orders not to advance further consolidated & remained there until the following event. During the afternoon two orders were recd to attack but had been cancelled — Slightly. Very little shelling.	
"	11-10-18	15.20	The Batt. was relieved by the WORCESTER (2nd Div.) & marched back to HENNECOURT where it was billeted in Railway huts.	
HENNECOURT	12-10-18		Fine. During the morning the Batt. cleaned up. 14:30 h. the Batt. moved to SERAIN arriving into Billets at 18.30. The Billets were in fair condition, but the men & all horses still occupied by civilians.	

Army Form C. 2118.

WAR DIARY
or
INTELLIGENCE SUMMARY.
(Erase heading not required.)

Instructions regarding War Diaries and Intelligence Summaries are contained in F.S. Regs., Part II. and the Staff Manual respectively. Title pages will be prepared in manuscript.

Place	Date	Hour	Summary of Events and Information	Remarks and references to Appendices
SERAIN	13-10-18		Sunday. fine. The C.O. addressed the Batt. Voluntary Church Service	
"	14-10-18		fine. The Brigadier addressed the Batt. — expressing his admiration of the way the Batt. fought & displayed themselves under most trying conditions. Baths & other Batt. arrangements	
"	15-10-18		Wet. Coys. at the pond of Our Coys. Baths in the afternoon.	
"	16-10-18		fine. C.O. inspected Companies. The Brigade moved to MONTREUX Ett. in reserve to the 5th Div. — Billets — Railway tunnels & cellars.	
"	17-10-18		Wet. The Brigade moved to the vicinity of FERMES farm in the afternoon & occupied sunken roads to	
	18-10-18	03.20	Zero hour until 09 o/clock — fine. The Batt. necessitation followed C.Bown. The Battal. proceeded to C.Bown + took up a position along Railway Embankment N. of SAZNN experiencing great difficulty in crossing the River SELLE on account of the enemy's M.G. fire.	
		0	The Batt. followed up the advance of the 95th Bde. with the KWORCESTERS on the Right & 15 WARWICKS on the left	

WAR DIARY
or
INTELLIGENCE SUMMARY.

(Erase heading not required.)

Army Form C. 2118.

Place	Date	Hour	Summary of Events and Information	Remarks and references to Appendices
		D	The Battalion Brigade formed thus: the 5th Gord's the Scots attacked Neighboured the railway of main LECOUVRE-BAZUEL Rd immediately WEST of BAZUEL. B. Coy. Right Front. C. " Left " A. " Left Support. D. " Reserve. The battalion suffered with 4 officer casualties — 2/LT. WOODWARD (C Coy) + 2/L H.M. SEARLE (B Coy) being severely wounded. During the day much inconvenience was caused by snipers from the Cliffs during the night the Coys moved forward c Coy who moved to Treesfield front in the front line along the Railway N. of BAZUEL to R by R.W. front early evening Rain — wet durant day.	
In the Line	24-10-18	05.30	A B Coys under Lt. F.J. Lovell advanced except the line of the R. RICHEMONT — 300 yds NORTH of B Coy front of peaceful invitation to advancing 250 stiff M.G. fire was encountered after Brilliant dashwork the Germans were soon put to flight, the rear line stiffening the Coy, retires accordingly to orders.	

WAR DIARY
or
INTELLIGENCE SUMMARY.
(Erase heading not required.)

Army Form C. 2118.

Instructions regarding War Diaries and Intelligence Summaries are contained in F. S. Regs., Part II. and the Staff Manual respectively. Title pages will be prepared in manuscript.

Place	Date	Hour	Summary of Events and Information	Remarks and references to Appendices
IN THE LINE	20-10-18		Except for desultory shelling earlier in the day this was the situation during the night. Capt. B 2nd Manchesters relieved Capt. B in the front line, after which B. Coy closed up to the Right Coy occupying line opposite [illegible] + Coy reduced platoon of the 2nd Manchesters.	
			Wet. Periodic shelling throughout the day.	
		07.00	Under a creeping barrage 150 meters deep, under 2/Lt V. Scroggie with 2nd Manchesters E and the left advancement formed the objective of yesterday. Stiff resistance was met with at first — but after stubborn fighting the enemy was expelled + withdrew towards Epehelle. Con. of the consolidation took place. This post was occupied by 2 sections of A Coy. Throughout the day enemy fire was maintained upright + firmness by Lts Stewart + Seller. Relief to 50 men dead.	
		20.00	The Batt was relieved — A.R+D bays by the remainder of the 2nd Manchester Rgt by 1 Coy.	
S. HENIN	21-10-18		The ½ LESTER Bar. — The Batt moved by trucks. Remainder occupying billets in outskirts of town.	
	22-10-18		Wet. Reveille 9:00 hrs. — Change of equipment. Inspection of theft 4/20 men. Wet. Baths.	
		23.00 hrs	The Batt moved off to Railway Cutting West of BAZUEL.	

WAR DIARY
or
INTELLIGENCE SUMMARY.
(Erase heading not required.)

Army Form C. 2118.

Place	Date	Hour	Summary of Events and Information	Remarks and references to Appendices
IN THE LINE	22.10.15		Quiet day.	
		01.20	Zero hour for attack by 3rd & 4th Armies. Dispositions of Battn. & Brigade:	
			1st Brigade Lt Cols 1st Bn.	
			2nd "	
			3rd "	
			4th " & Trench Mjrs.	
		02.10	The battalion approached behind 1st Bn.	
			Supports kept fifty A.D. Coys. B. Coy. Reserve. After advancing 200 staff[?] encountered and[?] and received rifle & M.G. fire & came under heavy Artillery fire. The supplies to enemy B.G. Jno shown heavy situation by Maj[?] went at the last dash of Pte Miles ____ C. Coy who arrived by himself taking all available cover & picked up ____ of twenty to kill & ____ ____ being ____ for our ____ ten prisoners further ____ the Bombing and another B. J. Co ____ The Company & advance ____ enabled the Company to advance to ____ up 16 Germans & many prisoners. After this the advance was able to be continued by C. Coy who being greatly delayed	

WAR DIARY
or
INTELLIGENCE SUMMARY.
(Erase heading not required.)

Army Form C. 2118.

Instructions regarding War Diaries and Intelligence Summaries are contained in F. S. Regs., Part II. and the Staff Manual respectively. Title pages will be prepared in manuscript.

Place	Date	Hour	Summary of Events and Information	Remarks and references to Appendices
In the line	24-10-18	09.15	Bn. the Bn. was relieved by the K.O. Scottish Rifles L.I. & the Wiltshires Bn. arrived at FLAQUET BRIAQUT, moving back to concentrate at an wda. arriving at billets at 20.00.	
POMMEREUIL	25-10-18		Bn. Officers & men in village. Coys. clearing of inhabitants.	
"	26.10.x		Bn. Village shelled during early hours from enemy A.G. near O.C. Coy	
"	27 10-18		Line – Village intermittently shelled with gas shell. Coys under 0.0 Coys	
"	28 10.18		Line	Do	Do
"	29 10.18		Line	Do	Do
"	29 10.18		Line	Do	Do
"	30 10.18		Line	Do	Bn. billets changed
			day at Q.M. Stores	
MAI GARNI	31.10.18		Bn relieved of YORKS B Coy Right front. D Coy Front O Coy Support front. Counter attack. 'A' Coy to Mouvres. Relief completed by 16.30	
"	"			

WAR DIARY
or
INTELLIGENCE SUMMARY.
(Erase heading not required.)

Army Form C. 2118.

Place	Date	Hour	Summary of Events and Information	Remarks and references to Appendices
			Went in to G. Reserve.	
			D Coy. not in Line at JACQUET MILL & "CARDE MILL" with stubborn fighting till 11am when A & B Coys of Foresters to their immediate left assisted FORESTERS who were hard pressed BRIGADE sent B Coy to the flank of C Coy. B & C Coys endeavoured to get into touch with a gap in my left & LEVEQUE WOOD & wall N.E. edge met with sharp resistance from M.G. fire & suffered a flank. After several hours of steady advance & fighting these Coys managed to get most of their positions, when orders were received to attack in S.E. direction. The attack took place at 16.41 h. when no resistance was met with & line was established along road running N.E. from FORESTERS H.Q. - MALCHAIRN. A Coy had still fighting along road running S.W. from FORESTERS H.Q. - BAZUEL in conjunction with the 1/5 LEICESTERS. Not being all I needed successfully positions at FORESTERS H.Q. the Coy received order to move to BATT H.Q. at FORESTERS H.Q. - hence to proceed along road to said FORESTER H.Q. should by that time have been clear of it. To take of a position in support of B & D Coys. During the night our losses were heavily shelled.	

A6945 Wt. W14422/M1106 35,000 12/16 D. D. & L. Forms/C. 2118/14.

Army Form C. 2118.

WAR DIARY
or
INTELLIGENCE SUMMARY.
(Erase heading not required.)

Instructions regarding War Diaries and Intelligence Summaries are contained in F. S. Regs., Part II. and the Staff Manual respectively. Title pages will be prepared in manuscript.

Place	Date	Hour	Summary of Events and Information	Remarks and references to Appendices
			WEEKLY STATES	
			WEEK ENDING / TOTAL RATIONED / ANIMALS / VEHICLES 2 wheel 4 wheel	
			5.10.18 562 54 4 14	
			12.10.18 460 39 4 14	
			19.10.18 583 58 4 14	
			26.10.18 564 56 (plus 7 aux) 4 14	
			CASUALTIES	
			OFF. O.R.	
			5/10/18 1 9 Killed in action	
			" " 42 Wounded in action	
			" " 1 Missing	
			6/10/18 ... 5 Killed in action	
			" 1 4 Wounded in action	
			" ... 1 Died of wounds	
			7/10/18 ... 7 Wounded in action	
			" ... 1 Died of wounds	
			" ... 1 Wounded (at duty)	
			" ... 4 Wounded in action	
			8/10/18 ... 10 Killed in action	
			9/10/18 2 33 Wounded in action	
			" ... 1 Died of wounds	
			" ... 2 Missing	
			10/10/18 ... 1 Killed in action	
			" 4 30 Wounded in action	
			11/10/18 ... 1 Wounded (S.I.)	
			" ... 1 Died of wounds	
			OFF. O.R.	
			15/10/18 ... 4 Died of wounds	
			18/10/18 ... 4 Killed in action	
			" 2 43 Wounded in action	
			" ... 1 Missing	
			19/10/18 ... 1 Killed in action	
			" ... 11 Wounded in action	
			" ... 3 Died of wounds	
			" ... 3 Missing	
			20/10/18 ... 4 Wounded in action	
			23/10/18 ... 6 Killed in action	
			" 2 37 Wounded in action	
			" ... 2 Died of wounds	
			24/10/18 ... 5 Killed in action	
			" ... 1 Wounded in action	
			" ... 2 Missing	
			26/10/18 ... 2 Died of wounds	
			HOSPITAL	
			ADMITTED	
			O. O.R.	
			0 34 during month	
			DISCHARGED	
			O. O.R.	
			0 8 during month	

WAR DIARY
INTELLIGENCE SUMMARY.
(Erase heading not required.)

Army Form C. 2118.

Place	Date	Hour	Summary of Events and Information	Remarks and references to Appendices

COURSES

		M.E.	O.R.			OFF.	O.R.	
	4.10.18	4	To XIII Corps L.G. Course		24.10.18		1	To 4th Army Signal School
	"	1	" Bombing Course		"		1	To G.H.Q. L.G. and Mobile Mortar School
	"		Stoke Mortar Course		29.10.18		1	Reft. from 4th Army S.O.S. School
	"	4	" Inf. School (Lieut A.T.L.GREAR)		"	1		" XIII Corps Bombing School
	"	1	" S.O.S. School		"		1	L.G.
	"	1	" 4th Army Musketry School (Capt A.C.HALL)		30.10.18	1		" 4th Army Inf. School (Capt G.E.RATCLIFF)
	"	12	" Signal School		"		1	" Musketry School
	"	7	" 4th Army Infantry School (Capt G.E.RATCLIFF)		31.10.18		2	To 4th Army Gas School
	22.10.18	4	" XIII Corps L.G. School					
	"	1	" Bombing School					
	"	1	" Stokes Mortar School					

MOVES OF OFFICERS

	1/10/18	Capt F.E.FRANCILLON	To 75th Inf/Bde H.Q.		13.10.18	Lieut F.L.LOVELL	Joined for duty
	5.10.18	Lieut J.A.CARROLL	Reft. from leave to ENG.		14.10.18	2/Lt V.SCROGGIE	"
	6.10.18	Lieut G.W.E.SEAGO	Wounded in action		16.10.18	" R.J.A.JACKSON	Granted 14 days leave to ENG. 19.10.18 - 2.11.18
	7.10.18	2/Lt H.G.POWELL	Granted 14 days leave to ENG. (6-20/10/18)		17.10.18	" F.W.NORRIS	" 19.10.18 - 2.11.18
	"	Capt L.R.C.SUMNER, M.C.	From Senior Off. Course ALDERSHOT		18.10.18	Major G.R.CROUCH	" 20.10.18 - 3.11.18
	"	2/Lt H.R.H.MORRIS	"		"	2/Lt S.F.WOODWARD	Wounded in action
	8.10.18	2/Lt W.L.PALMER	Joined Bn. for duty		"	" H.H.SEARLE	"
	"	" S.F.WOODWARD	"		25.10.18	Lieut F.J.LOVELL	"
	"	" A.T.JACKSON	"		"	2/Lt H.BUSBY	"
	"	" W.H.ROBBINS	"		26.10.18	Capt G.HAWKINS	Joined for duty
	"	" E.G.TURNER	"		"	Lieut F.A.C.NEEDHAM	"
	"	Capt V.B.BINGHAM-HALL	Reft. from leave to ENG.		27.10.18	" C.L.P.GILSHENAN	"
	9.10.18	2/Lt H.H.SEARLE	Joined Bn. for duty.		"	2/Lt LE DE RIDDER	Granted 14 days leave to Hospital 29/10/18 - 12/11/18
	"	" H.BUSBY	"		27.10.18	" A.H.FEARMAN	To Hospital
	"	" N.JERRAM	"		28.10.18	" H.G.POWELL	Granted Extension of leave to 25.10.18. (25 Nov - Nov A/17/15 - 9.29.10.18)
	"	" G.H.WEST	"		29.10.18	" H.G.POWELL	Reft. from leave to ENG.
	"	Lieut J.A.CARROLL	Wounded in action		30.10.18	Capt C.R.GOOTE	Granted 14 days Special leave to ENG. (29.10.18 - 16.11.18)
	"	2/Lt A.J.COX	"		"	2/Lt R.S.BAKER	Granted 14 days leave to ENG. (1.11.18 - 15.11.18)
	10.10.18	Capt R.de M.ROGERS	"		"	" R.H.COYSH	Joined for duty
	"	2/Lt H.J.NORTHCOTT	"		31.10.18	Capt C.A.CLARK, M.C.(Chaplain)	" Aff. Bn.
	"	" H.R.H.MORRIS	"		"	2/Lt N.P.ANGELL	Joined for duty
	"	" W.L.PALMER	"				

1/5th Battn. Gloucestershire Regt.

WAR DIARY

VOL. XLIV.

Nov. 1918.

WAR DIARY
or
INTELLIGENCE SUMMARY.
(Erase heading not required.)

Army Form C. 2118.

Place	Date	Hour	Summary of Events and Information	Remarks and references to Appendices
In the line MALGRNI	1.11.18		Slight shelling during the day. Battalion had 7 casualties	
do	2.11.18		Brigade on right attacked and advanced their line slightly, the enemy retaliated on our right front by (B) causing us n 5 casualties. Later in the day enemy counterattacked regaining their lost ground. B Coy were obliged to relinquish an advanced post which they had occupied in the morning, to conform with the Lancashire Fusiliers on their right.	
do	3.11.18		The enemy heavily shelled our reserve Company (A) causing 7 casualties. Brigade on our right attacked again gaining their objective. Little retaliation by the enemy during the attack but a good deal later on in the day. We sustained 5 casualties from our Artillery who were shooting short.	
do	4.11.18		75th Brigade attacked at 06.15 hours, the objective being the town of LANDRECIES. Disposition 1/5th Gloucesters on the right 1/8th Warwicks on the left and 1/8th Worcesters in reserve	

WAR DIARY or INTELLIGENCE SUMMARY

Army Form C. 2118.

Place	Date	Hour	Summary of Events and Information	Remarks and references to Appendices
In the line	4.11.18		Disposition of Battalion. A Coy (right front) C Coy (left front) D Coy Moppers up, and B Coy in reserve. Objective was to reach the bank of the SAMBRE CANAL and if possible to bridge and cross it. The attack started in a thick mist which at first caused a little confusion owing to the close country, and A Coy became somewhat split up but B Coy moved up to the front line and the attack progressed successfully right to the canal bank, where a few of D Coy crossed. The WORCESTERS then came through us – crossed the canal and advanced through LANDRECIES followed by the Battalion who after moving south formed a defensive flank facing south. In this operation we captured about 350 prisoners, 3 Anti Tank Guns, 1 Field Gun, 1 Motor Ambulance, 1 Horse Ambulance, complete, and numerous Machine Guns. Our casualties were Capt H.J. Mallme and 2nd Lieut J SERODINE killed.	

WAR DIARY
or
INTELLIGENCE SUMMARY

Army Form C. 2118.

Place	Date	Hour	Summary of Events and Information	Remarks and references to Appendices
L. de ligne	4.11.18		2nd LIEUT JACKSON, LIEUT GILSHENAN, 2nd LIEUT POWELL and CAPT G HAWKINS were wounded. 12 O.R.'S killed and 49 wounded. In this operation we were protecting the flank of the 74th Brigade who had passed through early in the evening. The 32nd Division were on our right. Between 2000 & 22.30 hours, three enemy patrols were ound to be approaching "A" Coys posts - these were at once dealt with in a satisfactory manner and as a result, the enemy lost 4 prisoners & 4 M.G.s captured.	
" "	5.11.18		At stand-down this morning A Coy withdrew to the LANDRECIES - MAROILLES Road.	
		10.00	At 10.00 hours the Battalion moved off as the rear Battalion of the Brigade which followed the 74th Brigade. A position was reached on the crossroads at M.20.6.20.	
		12.00	(Map Ref: FRANCE 57.A 1/40,000) 1 Kilo S.E. of Le PRESAU at 1200 hours, where the Battalion halted & were billeted in barns nearby.	
	6.11.18		The Battalion remained in billets resting.	
	7.11.18	04.00	At 04.00 hours the Battalion moved off in column of route to the outpost line which was found through at 06.00 hours, 1 Kilo E. of MARBAIX.	
		08.00	An advanced guard was formed - B & D Coys in the van and A & C as	

WAR DIARY
INTELLIGENCE SUMMARY

Army Form C. 2118.

Place	Date	Hour	Summary of Events and Information	Remarks and references to Appendices
In the line	7.11.18		the moved with the whole forming advanced guard to the Brigade — a distance of 600x was obtained between the van & the main guards.	
			The advance was the main road AVESNES — MAUBEUGE on the Nouvelles cob roads of AVESNES. We were held up 1 mile E. of ST HILAIRE by a string line of enemy M.G.s at J.18 d.88 (Map Ref: 57 A 1/40000)	
			At dusk an outpost line was formed of about 2000x in width, with "C" coy on left, "D" in centre, "B" on right + "A" in reserve. This line extended from J.10 c.9.4.5, J.16 g.3 (Map Ref: 57 A 1/40000). The 32nd Division were on the Right & the 7th Brigade on the left.	
		2020	At about 20.00 hours the Battalion was relieved by the Kings Liverpool Regt + moved back into billets at MARBAIX, the last company arriving at 00.30 hours on 8th.	
	8.11.18	09.00	An advanced party consisting of 1 officer + 7 O.R. proceeded on bicycles to PREUX AU BOIS.	
		10.30	Battalion marched out of MARBAIX at 10.30 hours travelled PREUX AU BOIS at 15.45 hrs.	
			En passing through LANDRECIES the Battalion marched past the G.O.C. Division. The Brigade had a good + enthusiastic reception on making their stay in the civilian inhabitants showing their gratitude for their release by the 5th Brigade by	

WAR DIARY
or
INTELLIGENCE SUMMARY
(Erase heading not required.)

Army Form C. 2118.

Place	Date	Hour	Summary of Events and Information	Remarks and references to Appendices
PREUX AU BOIS	8.11.18		distributing tri-colour flags & flowers to the troops	
	9.11.18		Billets at PREUX AU BOIS. The day was given over to cleaning up & resting	
	10/11/18	10.00	Words. Church Parade at 10.00 hours	
			XIII Legation unit Company arrangements	
		14.00	Sanitary men under the M.O. at 14.00 hours. Inspection	
		14.30	Demonstration of gas treatment	
	11/11/18	09.00	Works. The Battalion cleared woods in the vicinity from 09.00 to 12.00 hours	
			Signallers under the Signalling Supervisor for instruction	
		09.15	New draft inspected by the C.O. at 09.15 hours	
	12/11/18	09.00	Inspection each Company mounted a Guard strictly instructed in Ammunition dry rifle cleaning - a Platoon lying 5 to 7 in the vicinity. A.A. gun dismounted Companies at disposal of O.C. Companies for rifle exploration, platoon drill,	
			games etc. from 09.00 - 12.30 hours	
		14.00	N.C.O.s under instruction & full support for instruction from 14.00 - 16.00 hours	
	13/11/18	09.00	An advance party of 1 officer & 50 O.R. proceeded on cycles to LE CATEAU as billeting party	
		10.00	The Battalion moved off at 10.00 hours & arrived LE CATEAU at 13.15 hours.	

WAR DIARY
or
INTELLIGENCE SUMMARY.

(Erase heading not required.)

Army Form C. 2118.

Place	Date	Hour	Summary of Events and Information	Remarks and references to Appendices
LE CATEAU	14/11/18	09.00	Work. Washing & cleaning of equipment 0900-11.00 hours	
			Cleaning of billets 11.00-12.00 hours	
			Returns under company arrangements 12.00-12.30 hours	
	14.15	N.C.O.s under orderly full Sergeant for instruction 14.15-15.15 hours	
			Games & football in the afternoon	
	15/11/18	09.00	Work. Platoon Drill P.T., Arms Drill 0900-11.00 hours	
			Specialist training, Arms Drill 11.00-12.15 hours	
			Baths during the morning & afternoon. Entertainment to all officers by the R.E. Division	
	14.00	Company Commanders conference at 14.00 hours	
	16/11/18	09.00	Work. Close order drill V.T. gymnastic 0900-12.30 hours	
	14.00	Sanitary men under Sanitary Sergeant for instruction at 14.00 hours	
	14.15	N.C.O.s under orderly full Sergeant for instruction 14.15-15.15 hours	
			In the afternoon stables inspection by the M.O. Inspection of arms & gas equipment	
			Sports Committee meeting at 15.00 hours	
			Church parade in the Theatre at 12.15 hours	
	17/11/18		Inspection of billets by the C.O. after parade	

Army Form C. 2118.

WAR DIARY
or
INTELLIGENCE SUMMARY.
(Erase heading not required.)

Instructions regarding War Diaries and Intelligence Summaries are contained in F. S. Regs., Part II. and the Staff Manual respectively. Title pages will be prepared in manuscript.

Place	Date	Hour	Summary of Events and Information	Remarks and references to Appendices
LE CATEAU	18/11/18	09.00	Work. Route march at 09.00 hours about 7 miles. Games were played during a long halt half way.	
		14.15	N.C.O's labor march off pull inspect for instruction at 14.15 hours	
			A battalion rowdon's shop has been opened	
	19/11/18	09.00	Work. N.T. & games from 09.00 – 09.45 hours.	
			Saluting Drill 09.45 – 10.30 hours	
			Platoon & Company Drill 10.30 – 11.30 hours	
			Lecture in the Theatre by the M.O. at 11.45 hours	
			Signallers under the S.O. for instruction	
			A large number of new officers arrived. Meeting of the Sports Committee at 12.00 hours.	
	20/11/18	09.00	Work. "A" & "B" Companies worked on salvage	
			"C" & "D" carried out N.T. & games from 09.00 – 09.45 hours	
			Company Drill 09.45 – 10.30 hours	
			Lewis Gun instruction 10.30 – 11.45 hours. Instructors & Companies at O.C. Companies discretion.	
			"C" company on Zero's Gun Range. Signallers under the S.O. for instruction.	
		11.45	Lecture by the C.O. on Educational Scheme & Demobilisation at 11.45 hours.	

Army Form C. 2118.

WAR DIARY
or
INTELLIGENCE SUMMARY.
(Erase heading not required.)

Instructions regarding War Diaries and Intelligence Summaries are contained in F. S. Regs., Part II. and the Staff Manual respectively. Title pages will be prepared in manuscript.

Place	Date	Hour	Summary of Events and Information	Remarks and references to Appendices
LE CATEAU	24/11/18	09.00	Work — A + B companies worked on salvage.	
			"D" Company on Rifle Range 09.00 - 12.30 hours	
			"C" Company - N. 7 + games 09.00 - 09.45 hours	
			Lewis Gun Range 09.45 - 12.30. Remainder of Company at the disposal of O.C. Company	
		10.00	Inspection of transport by Brigade Commander + O.C. Divisional Train at 10.00 hours	
	25/11/18	09.00	Work — C + D companies worked on salvage.	
			"A" Company on Rifle Range 09.00 - 12.30 hours	
			"B" Company — N. 7 + games 09.00 - 09.45 hours	
			Lewis Gun Range 09.45 - 12.30 hours. Remainder of company at the disposal of O.C. Company.	
			Inspection of "C" Company's rifles by Armourer Sergeant.	
	26/11/18	09.00	Work — "C + D" Companies worked on salvage.	
			"A" Company — Lewis Gun Range from 09.00 - 11.00 hours	
			Lewis Gun Range 11.00 - 12.30 hours.	
			"B" Company — at disposal of O.C. Company 09.00 - 11.00 hours Lewis Gun Range 11.00 - 12.30 hours	

Army Form C. 2118.

WAR DIARY
or
INTELLIGENCE SUMMARY.
(Erase heading not required.)

Instructions regarding War Diaries and Intelligence Summaries are contained in F. S. Regs., Part II. and the Staff Manual respectively. Title pages will be prepared in manuscript.

Place	Date	Hour	Summary of Events and Information	Remarks and references to Appendices
LE CATEAU		12.00	Inspection by the C.O. of Signalling Equipment & Tools, Armourers Panniers Tools at 12.00 hrs.	
			Inspection of D Company's rifles by the Armourer Sergeant.	
			Result of the Batin - Company Cross Country Run for the week :-	
			Finished Ration Strength Percentage	
			1st B. Company 61 107 57.00	
			2nd D. Company 45 98 45.91	
			3rd A. Company 48 107 44.85	
			4th C. Company 29 107 26.16	
	24/11/18	11.00	Church Parade in the Zanawhie Zola Theatre 11.00 hours.	
			Inspection of billets by the C.O. after church parade.	
			Inspection of "A" Company's rifles by the Armourer Sergeant.	
	25/11/18	09.00	Work. A & B Companies worked on salvage.	
			C Company on Rifle & Lewis gun Ranges from 09.00 - 12.30 hours	
			D Company at disposal of O.C. Company from 09.00 - 12.30 hours	
			Inoculation of 20 E. Company men by the M.O.	

Army Form C. 2118.

WAR DIARY
or
INTELLIGENCE SUMMARY.
(Erase heading not required.)

Place	Date	Hour	Summary of Events and Information	Remarks and references to Appendices
LE CATEAU			Result of Saturday's matches in the Inter-Platoon football competition:—	
			1 Platoon v 3 Platoon 1 – 6 goals	
			6 " v Signallers 4 – 3	
			7 " v Transport Drivers 0 – 3	
			15 " v Band 1 – 0	
			9 " v 11 Platoon 9 – 2 Played on 27th November	
	26/11/18	0900	Work. "A" + "B" Companies worked in salvage.	
			"C" Company at disposal of O.C. Company	
			"D" Company on Rifle + Lewis Gun Ranges from 0900 – 12.30 hours	
			Divisional Baths for all but "A" + "B" Companies	
	29/11/18	0900	Work. C + D Companies worked in salvage. A + B Companies carried out half hour P.T. + half an hour Company Drill during the morning.	
			A comparison of arms was held by Major Storrock at 1315 hours.	
			Result of today's matches in XIII Bde Inter-Company Competition	
			"A" 6 of 4 – HQ 1 goal	
			"B" 6 of 7 goals – "D" 6 of 3 goals.	

WAR DIARY
INTELLIGENCE SUMMARY.
(Erase heading not required.)

Army Form C. 2118.

Place	Date	Hour	Summary of Events and Information	Remarks and references to Appendices
LE CATEAU	28/11/18		Result of the book house Competition held during Sept & Oct last.	
			1st "B" Coy 25 marks	
			2nd "C" Coy 24 marks	
			3rd "D" Coy 22 marks	
			4th { A Coy 20 marks	
			{ HQ	
	29/11/18	10.50	A & B Coys worked on salvage for 4 hours.	
			D Coy on rifle & LG ranges.	
			C Coy at O.C. Coys disposal.	
			Result of XIII Corps Inter Company Competition D Coy 3 — C Coy 1 goal	
CARNIERES	29/11/18	16.45	Battn moved to CARNIERES in the rain, B Band A & D HQ Details billeting there during the afternoon. Distance marched about 10 miles.	
"	30.11.18	09.00	Morning devoted to cleaning billets kits and the erection of temporary athletic tracks. Company Drill, PT and games were also carried out.	

Army Form C. 2118.

WAR DIARY
or
INTELLIGENCE SUMMARY.
(Erase heading not required.)

Instructions regarding War Diaries and Intelligence Summaries are contained in F. S. Regs., Part II. and the Staff Manual respectively. Title pages will be prepared in manuscript.

Place	Date	Hour	Summary of Events and Information	Remarks and references to Appendices

WEEKLY STATES

WEEK ENDING	TOTAL RATIONED	ANIMALS	VEHICLES 2 wheeled	4 wheeled
2.11.18	646	59	4	14
9.11.18	574	62	4	14
16.11.18	658	63	4	14
23.11.18	667	56	4	14
30.11.18	642	62	4	14

CASUALTIES

Date	O.	O.R.	
2.11.18		11	Wounded
3.11.18		1	Returned in action
"		4	Died of wounds
"		10	Wounded
"			Wounded (N.F. duty)
4.11.18	2	16	Killed in action
"	4	42	Wounded
"		2	Accid. wounded
"		1	Wounded (at duty)
6.11.18		1	Died of wounds
7.11.18		1	Died of wounds
"		7	Wounded
8.11.18		1	Died of wounds
12.11.18		1	Died of wounds

HOSPITAL

Date	ADMITTED during month		DISCHARGED during month	
	OFF. O.R.		OFF. O.R.	
	3 27		1 2	

COURSES

Date	O.	O.R.	
14.11.18		1	½ GHQ L.G School (McHaccore)
"		1	To XIII Corps Lewis School
9.11.18	1		Rept from Raye's Course BMS (Capt White)
10.11.18			Rept from 4th Army Musk. School (Capt McNeill)
12.11.18		1	To GHQ L.G School
13.11.18		4	To XIII Corps L.G. Rly. School
14.11.18		3	Rept from GHQ L.G School (Plte McCoare)
"		2	Rept from XIII Corps Inf School
"		1	Rept from GHQ L.G School
15.11.18	1	1	Rept from XIII Corps Inf School (Lieut ATL.GREAR)
17.11.18		1	Rept from 4th Army Inf School
21.11.18		4	Rept from XIII Corps L.G Rly School
25.11.18		2	To Corps Course (Pract. Fireworks)
"		1	Rept from XIII Corps Repeat School

WAR DIARY
or
INTELLIGENCE SUMMARY.
(Erase heading not required.)

Army Form C. 2118.

Place	Date	Hour	Summary of Events and Information	Remarks and references to Appendices
			MOVES OF OFFICERS	
	2.11.18		2/Lt H.C. LODGE to Hospital sick.	
	6.11.18		Capt G.E. RATCLIFFE transferred to class Z/R. B-22.11.18	
	do		2/Lt F.W. NORRIS Rejd from leave to U.K.	
	7.11.18		Capt E.R.T. SUMNER M.C. to Hospital sick	
	do		Capt F.E. FRANCILLON Appt 2nd in Command HQ	
	8.11.18		Major G.R. CROUCH Rejd from leave to U.K.	
	do		2/Lt A.E. PRICE Joined Bn. for duty	
	do		2/Lt N.P. ANGELL Admitted to hospital sick	
	9.11.18		2/Lt A.E.W. BOLT Joined Bn. for duty	
	do		G.S. PARTRIDGE do do	
	10.11.18		Capt A.C. HILL appd O.C. "C" Coy.	
	14.11.18		2/Lt L.E. DE RIDDER Rejd from leave to U.K.	
	do		Capt A.C. HILL Granted 14 days leave to U.K. 16-30.11.18	
	16.11.18		2/Lt H.C. LODGE to ENGLAND, sick.	
	4.11.18		A.H. FEARMAN do do	
	15.11.18		2/Lt N.P. ANGELL Discharged from Hospital	
	do		" R.S. BAKER Rejd from leave to U.K.	
	do		" C.S. BARNETT Joined Bn. for duty	
	do		" A.H. YOUNG do	
	do		" C.L. SIMS do	
	19.11.18		" E.W. GODDARD do	
	do		" G.A. BRINKWORTH do	
	do		" E.A. BRESMAN do	
	do		" F.W. EVERALL do	
	20.11.18		Lieut W.H. COOMBS M.C. do	
	21.11.18		" A.T.L. GREAR Granted 14 days leave to U.K. 22.11.18 - 7.12.18	
	do		Capt B.B. KIRBY Joined Bn. for duty	
	23.11.18		2/Lt J.R. COSWAY do	
	25.11.18		Capt G.E. RATCLIFFE M.C. Rejd from leave to U.K.	
	26.11.18		" C.R. COOTE D.S.O. Granted 14 days leave to U.K. 28/11/18 (W.O. AG4F.4/16.11.18)	
	29.11.18		Lieut P.A. MORFEY M.C. Granted 14 days leave to U.K. 1-15.12.18	

Y. Francillon Capt
for Major.
Comdg. 1/6 Bn. Glost. Regt.

CONFIDENTIAL.

1/5" GLOUCESTERSHIRE REGT.

WAR DIARY.

FOR MONTH OF DECEMBER. 1918.

VOL. 42.

1st JAN. 1919.

WAR DIARY
or
INTELLIGENCE SUMMARY.

(Erase heading not required.)

Army Form C. 2118.

Place	Date	Hour	Summary of Events and Information	Remarks and references to Appendices
CARNIERES	1.12.18	11.30	Voluntary Church Parade.	
		12.00	Inspection of billets by C.O.	
"	2.12.18	09.00	'C' and 'D' Coys carried out salvage work, working for 6 hours. 'A' & 'B' " PT, Games, Coy & Platoon Drill, Musketry. Result of XIII Corps Inter Coy Competition :- B Coy 2 goals A Coy 1 goal	
"	3.12.18	09.00	'C' and 'D' Coys continued salvage work, working for 6 hours. A & B Coys carried out training in PT, Games, Musketry, Guard Mounting and Coy lectures on Military subjects. B Coy also carried out Lewis Gun training	
"	4.12.18	13.30	His Majesty the King passed on foot through CARNIERES, the troops lining up on both sides of the road and cheering him.	
		09.00-11.00	Coys carried out 2 hours training	

Army Form C. 2118.

WAR DIARY
or
INTELLIGENCE SUMMARY.

(Erase heading not required.)

Instructions regarding War Diaries and Intelligence Summaries are contained in F. S. Regs., Part II, and the Staff Manual respectively. Title pages will be prepared in manuscript.

Place	Date	Hour	Summary of Events and Information	Remarks and references to Appendices
CARRIERES	5/12/18	0900	A + B Coys continued salvage work from C and D Coys respectively	
			C + D Coys carried out training in PT, Games & Close Order Drill	
			Lewis Gun range attached to C. Coy	
		1130	Lecture by Professor CROMMELIN on Astronomy to C. Coy?	
			The Battalion bathed during the day at AVESNES LES AUBERT	
"	6/12/18	0900	A + B Coys continued salvage work for 6 hours	
			C + D Coys carried out training in P.T. Games, Close Order Drill, Musketry	
			Lewis Gun Range allotted to C. Coy	
			An Advd N Board assembled at HQ Mess to audit the Canteen a/c	2/Lieut E B Kirkby MC Lieut W H Coombes 2/Lieut A R W Bolt
"	7/12/18	0700	A + B Coys continued salvage work for 4 hours	
			Rifle Range allotted to C. Coy. Lewis Guns Range to D. Coy.	
			Presentation of Medal Ribbons by the Divisional Commander	
		1020	C. Coy furnished 1 Off + 33 men as representative detachment	

Army Form C. 2118.

WAR DIARY
or
INTELLIGENCE SUMMARY.
(Erase heading not required.)

Instructions regarding War Diaries and Intelligence Summaries are contained in F. S. Regs., Part II. and the Staff Manual respectively. Title pages will be prepared in manuscript.

Place	Date	Hour	Summary of Events and Information	Remarks and references to Appendices
CARNIERES	8/12/18		Church Parade in R.M.T. hangar. Also service for Non conformists. Wesleyans & United Board.	
			Inspection of Billets by the C.O.	
			Result of XIII Corps Lewis Gun Competition. B Coy 1/5th Bord. Regt - 0 Gds. C Coy 1/8th Warwicks - 1	
"	9.12.18	09.00	C & D Coys continued salvage work from A & B Coys.	
			Lewis Gun Range is allotted to B Coy. Rifle Range to A Coy.	
			Presentation of Medal Ribbons by Divisional Commander.	
			A Coy furnished a representative detachment of 1 Off + 33 O.R.	
	10.12.18	09.00	C & D Coys continued salvage work	
			A & B Coys carried out training in Platoon Drill, P.T. + Games	
			Musketry, Company Drill	
			New Drafts Lewis Gunners handed over to L.G.O.	
			Companies re-organised into 4 Platoons forthwith.	

Army Form C. 2118.

WAR DIARY
or
INTELLIGENCE SUMMARY.
(Erase heading not required.)

Instructions regarding War Diaries and Intelligence Summaries are contained in F.S. Regs., Part II. and the Staff Manual respectively. Title pages will be prepared in manuscript.

Place	Date	Hour	Summary of Events and Information	Remarks and references to Appendices
CARNIERES	11/12/18	07.00	C + D Coys continued salvage work working for 2½ hours	
			A + B Coys carried out training in Platoon Drill, P.T. & General Musketry, Bombing Drill, Rapid Loading	
			The C.O. inspected A + B Coys on organization during the morning	
			The M.O. inspected the new draft men at Medical Room.	
"	12.12.18	07.00	A - B Coys continued salvage work working for 6 hours.	
			C + D Coys carried out training in subjects mentioned above	
			Officers daily classes under Capt LAXTON commenced today	
		09.00	The new draft were however paraded under L.C.O.	
"	13.12.18	07.00	A + B Coys continued salvage work	
		07.30	C + D Coys carried out training in the subjects mentioned above	
			The C.O. inspected C + D Coys on organization	
		11.30	The M.O. inspected C Coys for rawrecu	
			No 1 and 2 L Gunners of A + B Coys paraded under L.C.O.	

(A9(75) Wt W2358/P360 600,000 12/17 D. D. & L. Sch 822. Forms/C2118/15.

Army Form C. 2118.

WAR DIARY
or
INTELLIGENCE SUMMARY.
(Erase heading not required.)

Place	Date	Hour	Summary of Events and Information	Remarks and references to Appendices
CARNIERES	14/12/18	9.00	A and B Coys continued salvage work. C and D Coys continued training in the subjects previously mentioned. The MO inspected D.Coy, HQ Details & Transport Section for scabies.	
		10.00	Court of Inquiry assembled to enquire and report on accident which occurred during Salvage Operations. President Capt B.B. Kirby MC Members Lieut F.A.C. Needham 2nd Lieut J. Bryant.	
"	15/12/18	10.30	Church Parade in Hangar at CARNIERES. The CO inspected Billets after parade.	
"	16/12/18	10.05	The Battalion moved to CAMBRAI and billeted there.	

Army Form C. 2118.

WAR DIARY
or
INTELLIGENCE SUMMARY.
(Erase heading not required.)

Instructions regarding War Diaries and Intelligence Summaries are contained in F. S. Regs., Part II. and the Staff Manual respectively. Title pages will be prepared in manuscript.

Place	Date	Hour	Summary of Events and Information	Remarks and references to Appendices
CAMBRAI	17.12.18	0900	Companies carried out 3½ hours training under Company arrangements. Company & Platoon Drill, Arms Drill, P.T. & Games.	
"	18.12.18	0900	Companies employed the morning with Interior Economy and cleaning up Billets. Hand Lewis Gunners paraded for course of instructions under L.G.O.	
"	19.12.18	0900	All Companies carried out talarge work, working for 6 hours. Lewis Gun Class continued under L.G.O. Lecture by Lieut A.T.L. GREAR. Subject "The British Empire".	
"	20.12.18	0900	Companies carried out 3½ hours training in Company & Platoon Drill, P.T. and Games. Extended Order Drill etc.	
		1430	Lewis Gun Section bombers of C & D Coys paraded under L.G.O. for instruction.	

WAR DIARY
or
INTELLIGENCE SUMMARY.

(Erase heading not required.)

Army Form C. 2118.

Place	Date	Hour	Summary of Events and Information	Remarks and references to Appendices
CAMBRAI	21.12.18	09.00 hrs	Companies carried out 3½ hrs training in Company & Platoon Drill, P.T. Games etc. Rifles of all reinforcements joined since Dec. 1st 1918 inspected by Armourer Sergeant. Company Monthly Sports Championship for period Nov 20th – Dec 20th. "B" Coy. 18 marks; "D" Coy. 11 marks; "A" Coy. 10 marks; "C" Coy. 2 marks.	
"	22.12.18	09.15 hrs	Batt'n paraded for Divine Service held in Bde Cinema at 09.45 hrs. C.O. inspected billets after parade. Inter Platoon Football Competition. No. 9 Platoon NIL. Transport 3 goals.	
"	23.12.18		Companies carried out 2 hours training under Coy. arrangements. Baths allotted to the Batt'n from 09.00 hrs till 16.00 hrs.	
"	24.12.18	09.30 hrs	"D" Coy. paraded to be split up into Industrial Groups.	
"	25.12.18		XMAS DAY. Christmas Dinners at 15.00 hrs & 15.30 hrs. 1 Officer & 30 O.R.s per Coy. attended C. of E. Service in Cinema at 11.15 hrs. 14324. Pte. F.G. MILES "C" Coy. awarded the V.C. See attached.	

WAR DIARY
or
INTELLIGENCE SUMMARY.

Army Form C. 2118.

Place	Date	Hour	Summary of Events and Information	Remarks and references to Appendices
CAMBRAI	26.12.18		BOXING DAY - Payee Sports held in K.O.M.R.K	
"	27.12.18	09.00 hrs	All Companies continued Salvage Work working for 6 hours.	
"	28.12.18	09.00 hrs	Companies at disposal of Coy. Commanders from 09.00 hrs - 12.30 hrs. A + B. Coys. paraded to be split up into Industrial Groups.	
"	29.12.18	10.25 hrs	40 O.R's per Coy. paraded for C of E Service in Cinema at 11.00 hrs. Iron Rations returned to Q.M Stores.	
"	30.12.18	09.00 hrs	Companies carried out 3½ hrs training in Company Drill, Guard duties, P.T. + Games.	
"	31.12.18	09.00 hrs	Company Route Marches combined with Artillery Deployment, till 11.15 hrs. Company Route Marches 11.30 hrs - 12.30 hrs. A Court of Enquiry composed of Capt. L.E.C. SUMNER M.C., Capt A.C. HILL, + 1 Subaltern assembled at O.R. at 09.00 hrs to enquire into + report on accident sustained by 39220 Pte. PROUDFOOT. B. "C" Coy. (CONTINUED)	

Army Form C. 2118.

WAR DIARY
or
INTELLIGENCE SUMMARY. (CONTINUED)
(Erase heading not required.)

Place	Date	Hour	Summary of Events and Information	Remarks and references to Appendices
CAMBRAI	31.12.18	10.00 a.m.	B. Coy. attended W.R.S. 1 Officer + 30 O.R's paraded to attend Hooking of Warwick's Colours	

WEEKLY STATES.

WEEK ENDING	TOTAL RATIONED	ANIMALS	VEHICLES 2 WHEELED	4 WHEELED
7.12.18	636	57	4	14
14.12.18	792	57	4	14
21.12.18	817	57	4	14
28.12.18	783	57	4	14

CASUALTIES.

	O.	O.R.		HOSPITAL			DISCHARGED during month	
13.12.18		2	Accidentally Wounded.	Admitted during month			OFF.	O.R.
30.12.18	1		an Injured.	OFF.	O.R.		2	17
				3	52			

COURSES.

	O.	O.R.			O.	O.R.
1.12.18		3	3 o Fitting Course "N" S.A.P. Workshop MAUROIS.	20.12.18		1	Rejoined 25th Divnl. Signalling Course.
do.		2	2 o Fitting Course XIV Corps M.T. Co. No 1 LE CATEAU	do.		2	To Lewis & Vickers Guns OSCC Robery Slype
2.12.18		1	To THIRD Army School of Cookery CAMBOAI.	21.12.18		1	To First Army Signalling School.
7.12.18		1	To Blacksmith Course, 25th Aux. M.T. Workshop ST AUBERT.	22.12.18		2	Rejd. from Band C Sergt. Course
10.12.18		2	Rejd. from Fitting Course, Workshop MAUROIS.	26.12.18		1	To Workshop G. O. Y. C. /a attached Lincolnth
12.12.18		2	2 o Fitting Course, Attd. Heavy Repair Workshop PARIS.	28.12.18		1	To First Army Workshop.
13.12.18		1	To Electrician Course. XIII Corps M.T. Workshop. N° 1 LE CATEAU	29.12.18		1	To First Army Workshop.
14.12.18		4	Rejd. from 25th Divnl. Signalling Course.	30.12.18		1	Rejd. from Cookery Course BOHAIN
15.12.18		2	Rejd. from XIII Corps Anti-Gas, Blacksmith Course.	do.		1	To Artillery Course BOHAIN
				do.		1	2 Lieut. Sigmund Gunner TENEUR.

Army Form C. 2118.

WAR DIARY
or
INTELLIGENCE SUMMARY.
(Erase heading not required.)

Place	Date	Hour	Summary of Events and Information	Remarks and references to Appendices
			MOVES OF OFFICERS	
	1.12.18		Lt. Col. D. Lewis. D.S.O. M.C. Granted 14 days leave to U.K. 2-16.12.18.	
	do		Capt. E.A. Slack. M.C. (Chaplain) do. 3-17.12.18.	
	8.12.18		Capt. M.H. Anton. Joined Bn. for duty.	
	do		2/Lt. E.L. Ovenden M.C. Rejd. from duty at Donnerveil.	
	9.12.18		2/Lt. A.T.L. Brear. Rejd. from leave to U.K.	
	13.12.18		2/Lt. G.S. Barnett. To La Hospital (Accidentally Wounded).	
	14.12.18		Capt. A.S. Hill. Rejd. from leave to U.K.	
	15.12.18		2/Lt. A.E.W. Bolt. Admitted to Hospital	
	16.12.18		Capt. L.R.C. Sumner M.C. Discharged Hospital.	
	do		2/Lt. Qm. T. Dennis. Granted special leave to U.K. 16-30.12.18.	
	do		2/Lt. G.H. West. M.C. To Officers Rest House, Paris-Plage. 16-13/1/19.	
	17.12.18		2/Lt. A.T. Ogden. Joined Bn. for duty.	
	do		2/Lt. A.J. Gibbons. Joined Bn. for duty.	
	19.12.18		2/Lt. P.A. Morfey. M.C. Rejd. from leave to U.K.	
	do		2/Lt. P.E. Rendall. Joined Bn. for duty.	
	22.12.18		Capt. B.B. Kirby. M.C. Granted 14 days leave to U.K. 22.12.18-5.1.19.	
	do		Lt. A.T.L. Grear. To Boulogne. Duties as Burial Officer.	
	24.12.18		Capt. V.S. Bingham-Hall. M.C. To Hospital.	
	do		2/Lt. A.E.W. Bolt. From Hospital.	
	do		Capt. E.A. Clark M.C. Rejd. from leave to U.K.	
	26.12.18		4/Lt. S. Bryant. SOS Class 15 U.K. 26.12.18-9.1.19.	
	do		2/Lt. E.H. West. M.C. From Officers Rest House, Paris Plage.	
	28.12.18		Capt. N.H. Laxton. Gtd. 1 month Special leave to U.K. 28.12.18-27.1.19.	
	29.12.18		Capt. S.W. Culverhouse. Special Pay to duty.	
	29.12.18		Bt. Col. D. Lewis. D.S.O. M.C. Rejd. from Leave to U.K.	
	30.12.18		2/Lt. H.A. Cooke. Granted 14 days leave to U.K. 30.12.18-13.1.19.	

Lewis
Lt. Colonel,
Comdg. 1/5th Bn. Gloucestershire Regt.

Issued with C.R.Os.
DATED 27TH DECEMBER, 1918.

HONOURS AND AWARDS.

His Majesty the King has awarded the VICTORIA CROSS to the undermentioned :-

No. 17324, Private F.G. MILES, Glouc. Regt.

For conspicuous gallantry and splendid initiative in attack. On the 23rd October, 1918, during the advance against the BOIS L'EVEQUE, his Company was held up by a line of enemy machine guns in the sunken road near the MOULIN L. JACQUES. Private MILES, alone, and on his own initiative, made his way forward for a distance of 150 yards under exceptionally heavy fire, located one machine gun and shot the man firing the gun. He then rushed the gun and kicked it over, thereby putting it out of action. He then observed another gun firing from 100 yards further forward. He again advanced alone, shot the machine gunner, rushed the gun and captured the team of 8. Finally he stood up and beckoned on his Company, who, following his signals, were enabled to work round the rear of the line, and to capture 16 machine guns, 1 Officer and 50 Other Ranks.

The courage, initiative and entire disregard of personal safety shown by this very gallant private soldier was entirely instrumental in enabling his Company to advance at a time when any delay would have seriously jeopardised the whole operation in which it was engaged.

CONFIDENTIAL

1/5th Bn GLOUCESTERSHIRE REGIMENT.

WAR DIARY

For month of

JANUARY. 1919.

VOL. 43

WAR DIARY
or
INTELLIGENCE SUMMARY.
(Erase heading not required.)

Army Form C. 2118.

Place	Date	Hour	Summary of Events and Information	Remarks and references to Appendices
CAMBRAI	1-1-19	09.30	All Companies carried out Salvage work - working for 6 hours	
"	2-1-19	09.00	Battalion carried Salvage work working for 6 hours	
"	3-1-19	09.15	Companies continued Salvage Work working for 6 hours. Meeting held in Recreation Room at 14.15 hours to discuss proposed Battalion Society	
"	4-1-19	09.00	Companies carried out 3½ hours training in P.T. & Games, Leng & Platoon Drill etc	
"	5-1-19	10.30	Battalion paraded for Divine Service held in Bde Cinema at 11.00 hours. All Government rifles the handed in to Q.M. Stores	
"	6-1-19	09.15	Battalion paraded & marched to new Parade ground to carry out 3½ hours training including Batt'n Drill	

WAR DIARY
or
INTELLIGENCE SUMMARY.

(Erase heading not required.)

Army Form C. 2118.

Place	Date	Hour	Summary of Events and Information	Remarks and references to Appendices
CAMBRAI	7.1.19	09.15	Gas houses continued Salvage work, working for 10 hours	
	8.1.19	09.15	Battalion paraded & marched to training ground & carry out 3½ hours training including Batt/ Drill	
	9.1.19	09.15	Battalion paraded & marched to training ground to carry out 3½ hours training including Batt/ Drill	
"	10.1.19	09.15	Gas houses continued Salvage work, working for 10 hours	
"	11.1.19	09.15	Battalion paraded & marched to training ground to carry out 3½ hours training including Batt/ Drill. 1 Officer & 15 O.R. per Company & 15 O.R. from H Qrs. attended lecture in Cinema Hall at 19.30 hours by Mr RONALD GURNER B.A. on the subject of "Development & Nature of the British Empire"	

WAR DIARY
or
INTELLIGENCE SUMMARY.
(Erase heading not required.)

Army Form C. 2118.

Place	Date	Hour	Summary of Events and Information	Remarks and references to Appendices
CAMBRAI	12.1.19	09.15	Battⁿ marched to the Balloon from Dq 15 hours till 16.30 hours	
			Voluntary Ch^h of E. Service held in the Bde Cinema at 11.00 hours.	
			Competition lectured on "Demobilisation" by 2nd Lt. E. A. BRESMAN (Demob Officer)	
			Result of Bn^{el}. Cross Country Run	
			Teams:- 1st 1/9th YORKS. REGT. 1623 points	
			2nd 1/5th GLOUCESTER REGT. 1548 "	
			3rd 11th SHERWOODS. 1360 "	
"	13.1.19	10.20	Battⁿ paraded & marched to Training ground where the Battⁿ was inspected at 11.00 hours by the G.O.C. Brigade.	
"	14.1.19	10.15	Battⁿ paraded & marched to Training ground where the Battⁿ was reviewed at 11.00 hours by the G.O.C. Division.	
"	15.1.19	09.15	Work parties continued Salvage work & working for 6 hours	

Army Form C. 2118.

WAR DIARY
or
INTELLIGENCE SUMMARY.
(Erase heading not required.)

Place	Date	Hour	Summary of Events and Information	Remarks and references to Appendices
CAMBRAI	16.1.19	0915	Kaptions Colours Arranged. Football HQ v. C.Co. Result 4th class against HQ. Weather fine.	
	17.1.19	0915	Captains orders or charge. Football C.Co. versus B.Co.(95) HQ. I.M.15.19 C.Co. won 3-2 after a good game. Sinner heavy snow.	
			HQ's v 1st Warwicks v Warwick ground. Kicked off in snow 3-2. H.Q. played a good game and this is a great improvement after heavy faster body by C.Co. on previous day.	
	18.1.19	0915	Batt'n Bn interior Econ'y. Accounts audited by Capt KIRBY.MC Capt Ratcliff and 1/3rd troops. Morning also examined clothes. Capt. A.C. Hill Monopolised billets and A.C. congratulated on Cleann & filled.	
	19.1.19	1030	Church Parade held in the theatre. Day Fine. Football A.Co. 1st. Football A.Co v C.Co. (Friendly) A.Co Lost 2 goals Nil. Lovely my start.	
	20.1.19	0915	Route March RAMILLY CREVECOEURS CAMBRAI (Reflect 1/3/1910/) Football Transport v 1/8 Warwicks B.C. on stores ground. Transport won 5-0 Extremely good game. Pte B.MILLETT of Transport broke his knee	

(A9473) Wt W3256/P160 600,000 11/17. D. D. & L. Sch. 53a. Forms/C2118/15.

WAR DIARY
or
INTELLIGENCE SUMMARY.

(Erase heading not required.)

Army Form C. 2118.

Place	Date	Hour	Summary of Events and Information	Remarks and references to Appendices
	20.1.19		Ground very heavy from A Coy's Cross Country Run held by Thompson D Co came in out of about 500 starters. 2/Lt DeRIDDER came in 4th.	
	21.1.19		Companies carried Salvage in a thorough days. A & C Coy worked Salvage. C Co worked on Rifle range. Everton Ovens told between the 7. 9-11 am. Lie parade was very small	
	22.1.19		Co. NCO's on Salvage. Other work and training Games taken ? 6 men reported sick	
	23.1.19		A Bln worked on Salvage. Other work & training same as yesterday. 5 men reported sick. D Co played B Coy's H.Q. on the Island ground in Brigade Cup. D Co lost 3-nil	
	24.1.19		C & D Co on Salvage. Other work as per yesterday. 6 men reported sick	

WAR DIARY or INTELLIGENCE SUMMARY

Army Form C. 2118.

Place	Date	Hour	Summary of Events and Information	Remarks and references to Appendices
	25/1/19		A.R.B.Cn continues Salvage work. Others two Coys marched away to Coy parade. Relict Pass Rifle Range. One reported sick.	
	26/1/19		Same as yesterday. A Rfmn Singh was killed. 16 tollies by Plague. Sky full of Oxen.	
	27/1/19		Sunny. Stores held in Recreation Rm up to date. 133 all ranks have been demobilised. This includes 3 officers. Guns reported sick. Gun shell filling.	
	28/1/19		2 Baptisms, a confirmation Salvage. A lecture was given by Cap.t S. MOORE on smoke, and Recommendations were reported on the Wealter line. Still Snow or to frozen. 2 Confirmed or Inputs.	

Army Form C. 2118.

WAR DIARY
or
INTELLIGENCE SUMMARY.
(Erase heading not required.)

Instructions regarding War Diaries and Intelligence Summaries are contained in F. S. Regs., Part II. and the Staff Manual respectively. Title pages will be prepared in manuscript.

Place	Date	Hour	Summary of Events and Information	Remarks and references to Appendices
	29.1.19		2 Corporals Executed. 2 Corporals on fats. Weather very cold. 7 men reported sick.	
	30.1.19		2 Corporals on Subsays. 2 Corporals Executors. 8 men reported sick.	
	31.1.19		Same as yesterday. 8 men reported sick. 15 men and Officer men for demobilisation. Total made demobilised to date 5 Officers 180 men.	

WEEKLY STATES.

WEEK ENDING	TOTAL RATIONED	ANIMALS	VEHICLES 2 WHEELED	4 WHEELED
4 - 1 - 19	801	60	4	14
11 - 1 - 19	811	59	4	14
18 - 1 - 19	781	55	4	14
25 - 1 - 19	738	55	4	14

Army Form C. 2118.

WAR DIARY
or
INTELLIGENCE SUMMARY.
(Erase heading not required.)

Summary of Events and Information

CASUALTIES.

NIL.

HOSPITAL.

Admitted during month	
OFF	OR
-	13

Discharged during month	
OFF	OR
-	1

COURSES.

Date	OFF	OR	Course			OFF	OR	
3.1.19	-	1	To Painting Sign. Drilling Coy. SAVY	3.1.19		-	1	Rept from Drilling Coy. ROUBAIX
5.1.19	-	1	To 3rd Army R.T. School Assa	9.1.19		-	1	Rept from 1st Army Signalling School
9.1.19	-	2	To 3rd Army Workshops AUBIN ST VAAST	15.1.19		-	1	Rept from Ind. Spouse Coy. TENEUR
do	-	-	To 25th Divl Signal School CAMBRAI	16.1.19		-	1	Rept from 7.6th Coy. MAUROIS
10.1.19	-	2	To 352 E.&M. Coy. RE. BEAUVAL	18.1.19		-	1	Rept from 87th Gordon RAF BOURSIES
11.1.19	-	4	To 200th Coy. R.A.S.C.	20.1.19		-	2	Rept from 200th Coy. RASC
do	-	1	To 253 E.&M. Coy. R.E. LA PLAQUE	23.1.19		-	2	Rept from Heavy Repair Workshop PARIS
12.1.19	-	1	To 87th Squadron R.A.F. Bourses	24.1.19		-	1	Rept from 7 Wireless Coy MARKOIS
13.1.19	-	1	To Foundry Coy. ST OMER					
14.1.19	-	2	To Carpentry Coy. Mine Elect Camp CAMBRAI					
do	-	1	To Telegraph Coy. ORIVSBAL					
do	-	1	To Survey Coy. BERUCHEM					
15.1.19	-	1	To 3rd Army Bomb School Buxielle-CHATEAU					
17.1.19	-	1	To 35th Arm.(Relief) Coy. HAVRE					
21.1.19	-	1	To P.U. R.T. School HARDELOT PLAGE					
22.1.19	-	1	To Bricklayers Course, 21st Divn School					
25.1.19	-	2	To XIII Corps Workshop Sch. CAVIDRY					

Army Form C. 2118.

WAR DIARY
or
INTELLIGENCE SUMMARY.

(Erase heading not required.)

Instructions regarding War Diaries and Intelligence Summaries are contained in F. S. Regs., Part II, and the Staff Manual respectively. Title pages will be prepared in manuscript.

Place	Date	Hour	Summary of Events and Information	Remarks and references to Appendices
			MOVES OF OFFICERS.	
	2.1.19		Lt. V/QM T. Dennis. Regt. from leave to U.K.	
	7.1.19		Capt. B.B.Kirby M.C. Rejd from leave to U.K.	
	8.1.19		Capt. M.St.C. Hamilton. Regt. from leave to U.K.	
	do.		2/Lt. C.L. Ovenden. M.C. granted 14 days leave to U.K.	
	12.1.19		Capt. F.E. Francillon. Sanction 1 month officers leave to U.K.	
	15.1.19		2/Lt. G.L. Sims. To 3rd Army Chemical Sch. Auxi-le-Chateau	
	16.1.19		Major. E.R. Crooke. Rejd from leave to U.K.	
	19.1.19		Lieut. P.A. Morfey M.C. To Dispersal Area for Demobilization	
	21.1.19		Capt. R.C. Hill. To Dispersal Area for Demobilization	
	27.1.19		Lieut. F.A.C. Needham. To Dispersal Area for Demobilization	
	29.1.19			

Stevens

Lieut-Colonel.
Comdg. 1/5th Bn Gloucestershire Regt.

1/5th Battn. Gloucestershire Regt.

WAR DIARY

Volume XLVIII

February, 1919.

Army Form C. 2118.

WAR DIARY
or
INTELLIGENCE SUMMARY.

(Erase heading not required).

Instructions regarding War Diaries and Intelligence Summaries are contained in F. S. Regs., Part II. and the Staff Manual respectively. Title pages will be prepared in manuscript.

Place	Date	Hour	Summary of Events and Information	Remarks and references to Appendices
CAMBRAI	1.2.19	09.15	2 Companies Continued Salvage in town area about	A 22 c 2.9
"	2.2.19		2 Coys Continued Education	
"	3.2.19	09.15	Sunday Voluntary Services. The CO inspected billets. Salvage continues as usual in town area. Education classes held between the hrs of 0845 - 1045	
"	4.2.19	09.15	Salvage and Education as usual. Billet placed out of bounds owing to infection. Nos of all ranks absentees up to 1st Feb 196	
"	5.2.19	09.15	Salvage and Education as normal. Lecture on South Africa at the 26' Gen Ambulance. Billet Canteen the same. The beer post cards stopped, beer is fairly good for health. Only Englisch beer Colas	
"	6.2.19	09.15	Salvage and Education as usual. And hours kept to as list. Hymn the Accounts. Weather very cold. Snow on the ground	
"	7.2.19	09.15	Salvage and Education as per yesterday	

WAR DIARY or INTELLIGENCE SUMMARY

Army Form C. 2118.

Place	Date	Hour	Summary of Events and Information	Remarks and references to Appendices
CAMBRAI	8.2.19	0915	Solange and Eunoucho as usuals. A lecture in the Theatre at 17.00 hrs. In terms by Lt SMS. BA Lutger. The ku false	
	9.2.19	0915	Battn of men warned for Rhine Bn's. 10 Officers and 200 men warned for Base. It will have remembered no one when on or off to 1st June, 1916. Church Services.	
	10.2.19	0915	Eunoucho classes held from 1055 - 1215hrs Solange, Four men as usual.	
	11.2.19	0915	Solange and Solange as per yesterday to see repokes due.	
	12.2.19	0915	Same as yesterday. Battn roll call.	
	13.2.19	0915	Same as yesterday for Parade Batt allotten to Coys	
	14.2.19	0915	Eunoucho Classes and Solange as usual	
	15.2.19		Eunoucho Classes as usual also Solange. Even repokee sick	

WAR DIARY or INTELLIGENCE SUMMARY

Army Form C. 2118.

Place	Date	Hour	Summary of Events and Information	Remarks and references to Appendices
CAMBRAI	16.2.19		Sunday. Church parade at 10.40 to other Church service in the Theatre	
"	17.2.19	9.15	Arranged as usual. B Coy was AWAITING (Alfred Stephenson) Branch Classes. 1/2 holiday to hour of Gordon 10 hits Branch.	
"	18.2.19	9.15	Salvage & Education. awaiting Gun Garden kit renew. Weather wet	
"	19.2.19	9.15	Salvage & Runah. C company B working near AWAITING	
"	20.2.19	9.15	Same as for yesterday	
"	21.2.19	9.15	Companies continue R&B Cos continue and moved to 1 C. C & D Cos continue and moved to 2 B.C. as close dry to salvage of men 30 mgs similar	
"	22.2.19	9.15	Salvage & Education as usual. For working No AWAIGHT. Many reported sick.	
"	23.2.19	9.15	Sunday. Voluntary Church Service in Recreation Room. The semi-final tie of Battn football competition was played on "B" 15 coveda ground 16/8 Woveda NB v 15/4 Yorks Reg "B" Coy. The former won by one goal to nothing.	

WAR DIARY
or
INTELLIGENCE SUMMARY.
(Erase heading not required.)

Army Form C. 2118.

Place	Date	Hour	Summary of Events and Information	Remarks and references to Appendices
	Dec 1919			
CAMBRAI	24	0915	Embarked on the parade for special training as per Brigade Programme. The Commanding Officer inspected No. 1 and 2 Coys to the Parks. The Divisional Baths were allotted to the Bath from 0835 hrs to 1215 hrs. Training continued in the Park.	
"	25		The semi-final of the Inter Coy football competition was played on ground behind Coy H.Q's. 18th R.B's v 1/5th Bath Warwicks Regt. "B" Coy. 18th R.B Warwicks won by 4 goals to nothing. Guns were reported active in the direction of Cambrai.	
"	26/12/0915		Nos 1 & 2 Coys continued training as per Army reported active	
"	27/12/0915		3-Nos. 1 & 2 Coys continued training in serum area. No. 1 Coy carried out training in the Park. Educational classes were held from 10.55 hrs to 12.35 hrs. Rugby football competition. 25th Division v 46th Division. The latter won by 9 points to nil. XIII Corps	

WAR DIARY
or
INTELLIGENCE SUMMARY.
(Erase heading not required.)

Place	Date	Hour	Summary of Events and Information	Remarks and references to Appendices
CAMBRAI	28/1/19	09¹⁵	Salvaging & towing carried out as usual. Lewis Guns class joined for the 1st by 2 new upholst. Orcks.	
	1/3/19	09¹⁵	Salvaging carried out as usual. Lewis Guns class by 1 opl. Oost. Orcks to be put forward as demo. at 2.30 hrs.	

WEEKLY STATES

WEEK ENDING	TOTAL RATIONED	ANIMALS	2-WHEELED	4-WHEELED
			VEHICLES	
1.2.19	700	58	4	14
8.2.19	591	55	4	14
15.2.19	533	56	4	14
22.2.19	434	53	4	14

CASUALTIES
Nil

HOSPITAL
ADMITTED during month
O. 0 O.R. 13

DISCHARGED during month
O. 0 O.R. 5

Army Form C. 2118.

WAR DIARY
or
INTELLIGENCE SUMMARY.
(Erase heading not required.)

Instructions regarding War Diaries and Intelligence Summaries are contained in F. S. Regs., Part II. and the Staff Manual respectively. Title pages will be prepared in manuscript.

Place	Date	Hour	Summary of Events and Information	Remarks and references to Appendices

COURSES

	O.	O.R.	
3.2.19		2	Rejd. from Fourth Army Workshops.
4.2.19		1	Rejd. from P.R.T. Schol, HARDELOT PLAGE
	1		2/Lt R.H. COYSH (& Batman) to Pure Chemistry
			Course, No 3 Schol., DOULLENS.
5.2.19		3	To Transport Course, 200 Coy R.A.S.C.
6.2.19		2	To Cookery Course, 2nd Army School of Cookery,
			CAMBRAI
"		1	Rejd. from Potters Course, VIII Corps M.T Coy,
			No1 LE CATEAU.
"		1	Rejd. from Transport Course, 200 Cy R.A.S.C.
10.2.19		1	Rejd. from School of Cookery, CAMBRAI
"		1	Rejd. from Riveting Course, R+E.F., OISSEL
11.2.19		1	Rejd. from Bombing Bugle Whistling Course,
			SAVY
11.2.19		1	To Cookery Course, ETAPLES
12.2.19		1	Rejd. from Lewis's Course, OISSEL
"		1	Rejd. from Forestry Course, ST SAENS
17.2.19		1	Rejd. from Telegraphy Course, 25th Div.t Schol.
19.2.19		1	To School of Cookery, ETAPLES
21.2.19		1	Rejd. from Cookery Course, CAMBRAI
23.2.19		1	Rejd. from Signalling (Wireless) Course,
			25th Div.t Schol.
24.2.19		1	Rejd. from Cinema Operator's Course,
			BEAUVAL
25.2.19		1	To Telegraphy Course, 25th Div.t Schol.

MOVES OF OFFICERS

1.2.19	2/Lt H.A. COOKE	Left Bn. for demobilization.
3.2.19	Lt. C.L. OVENDEN M.C.	Leave extended by W.O. to 3/2/19.
		(W.O. A.G. 4f Letter 29/1/19)
4.2.19	Capt. B.B. KIRBY M.C.	To 25th Div.t HQ. member of Advisory Board.
5.2.19	2/Lt. E.C. TURNER	Granted leave to PARIS 5-12.2.19
7.2.19	2/Lt. A.E. PRICE	Granted 14days leave to U.K. 8-22.2.19
"	2/Lt. G.H. WEST M.C.	Left Bn. for demobilization.
8.2.19	Capt. R.B. KIRBY M.C.	Rejd. from 25th Div.t HQ as Member of Advisory Board.
10.2.19	2/Lt. W.H. ROBBINS	To ENG. conducting party for demobilization.
15.2.19	Capt. F.E. FRANCILLON	Rejd. from leave to U.K.
"	2/Lt. E.C. TURNER	Rejd. from leave to PARIS
21.2.19	Capt. F.E. FRANCILLON	Left Bn. for demobilization.
"	Capt. G.F. RATCLIFFE M.C.	
23.2.19	Lieut. W.H. COOMBS M.C.	Granted leave to ROUEN 23-26.2.19
24.2.19	2/Lt. A.E. PRICE	Rejd. from leave to U.K.
"	Lieut. S. BRYANT, M.C.	Pending demobilization in U.K.
"	Lieut. C.L. OVENDEN M.C.	that offr. struck off strength on expiration of granted leave. (J.S.M.A. 1087 of 21/2/19)
26.2.19	Major L.R.C. SUMNER, M.C.	To ENG. conducting party for demobilization.

Ends H-t Col Glouces
Lieut-Colonel.

www.ingramcontent.com/pod-product-compliance
Lightning Source LLC
Chambersburg PA
CBHW081448160426
43193CB00013B/2408